Goodword Books Pvt. Ltd.
P. O. Box 3244, Nizamuddin P. O.,
New Delhi-110 013
E-mail: info@goodwordbooks.com
Printed in India
Illustrated by Achla Anand
First published 2005   Reprinted 2006
© Goodword Books 2006

www.goodwordbooks.com

FAVOURITE TALES FROM THE QURAN

TWO TALES:

Sleepers in the Cave
Two Gardens

Saniyasnain Khan

The Sleepers in the Cave

SURAH AL-KAHF 18:10-21

It was about A.D. 250, during the rule
of a Roman King Decius (Daqyanus),
that the teachings of the Prophet Isa
(Jesus) ﷺ were spread throughout the
region by his early followers.

The people there were not true believers, the moon was treated as a god and worshipped. But seven young men of a noble family accepted the new religion in Ephesus, an ancient city near the western coast of Turkey, whose ruins can still be seen. Decius took up arms against the new converts.

Due to their fearless preaching and willingness to give up everything so as to tread the right path, they were honoured with the high status of being near to Allah. When these young believers realised that the king's soldiers were about to capture them, they ran away from the town. They took refuge in a cave so as to escape the cruelty of the king.

8

As they ran, they prayed to Allah: "Our Lord! show us Your Mercy and save our lives!" They ran far into the wilderness, until they found a dark cave. They entered in it with great caution, and hoped that no one would guess that there was anyone inside. Then weeping, they all prayed to Allah for His help.

Allah heard their prayers and, when they lay down to rest, He caused a miracle to happen. With His supreme power over life and death, He made them fall into a deep sleep lasting about 300 years. Not once during this time did they awaken. They neither ate nor drank nor made any sound. They only turned from side to side in their sleep. Even their dog Qitmir joined them in their long slumber with his legs stretched out across the entrance to the cave. This cave was so placed that not even a ray of light could enter it. Allah

had also made it look so frightening
that, if anyone had come close to it, he
would have felt afraid and run away. It
was one of the wonders of Allah.

Time passed and the town they had left changed altogether. The cruel king had died and the present king had become a believer, a follower of the message of the prophet Isa عليه السلام. The king and the people were believers in Allah. During this period, Allah woke up the sleeping men. As they arose up from their long slumber and stretched their arms and legs, one of them wondered, "How long have we been

here?" They thought about it, then said, "We have been here for a day or part of a day." They did not realise that they had been sleeping there for about three centuries!

They felt very hungry, so one of them
crept out of the cave to fetch something
to eat. He reached the town and went to
a shop to buy some food.

He paid the shopkeeper with a silver coin. The shopkeeper was amazed to see such an old coin and suspected that this man might have found some old hidden treasure. So he took him to the king, who immediately recognised that he must be one of those men who had been lost for about three hundred years.

By order of the king, the date they were lost their names and other particulars had been engraved on a lead slab which was kept in the Royal Treasury. For this reason they also came to be known as the "men of the slab." When the slab was taken out, it was confirmed that these were the very men who had run away from the city to save their lives more than two centuries ago. They immediately became the centre of people's devotion. The new Roman King, Theodosus, himself went on foot to see them and seek their blessings. When these young men died, a place of worship was built at their cave as a memorial.

The story tells us that those who put their entire trust in Allah, will be helped by Him in unknown ways. The story is also intended to tell us that there really is life after death.

Two Gardens

Long long ago, there lived two friends.
One of them was a rich gardener, while
the other one was a poor farmer. The
gardener owned a huge plot of land. He
cultivated his land very ably and developed
it into two beautiful and blooming gardens.
They were full of flowers and all kind of
fruits, especially grapes and dates. The
vineyards were set about with palm trees
and watered by a running stream.

Whenever the gardener would visit his gardens, he would be thrilled by seeing trees laden with ripe fruits. His heart would be filled with pride and arrogance. He would think this was all a

result of his hard work and clever planning. He would ignore the fact that his entire fortune was actually a blessing from Allah. Without Allah's help, no one can achieve a single thing on this earth.

One day his friend, the poor farmer
visited him. The gardener took him around
his beautiful garden and proudly said to
him, "I am richer than you and my clan is
mightier than yours." Looking at his
gardens, he continued: "Surely this will
never perish!" Puffed up with the evil of

wealth he went on denying the Day of
Judgement: "Nor do I believe that the
hour of Doom will ever come."

Then he added: "Even if I return to my Lord, I shall surely find a better place than this." Little did he realize that all this was wishful thinking. When the poor farmer noticed that his friend was behaving in a wicked way, he tried to correct him. He added: "Have you no faith in Him who created you from dust, from a little germ, and fashioned you into a man?"

The poor man went on: "As for myself, Allah is my Lord, and I will associate no one else with Him."

He advised the gardener that instead of entering the garden proudly, he should have gone into it in all humility and should have said: "What Allah has ordained must surely come to pass: there is no strength except in Allah." "Though you see me poorer than yourself and blessed with fewer children," the farmer argued, "yet my Lord may give me a garden better than yours, and send down thunderbolts from heaven upon your vineyards, turning them into a barren waste, or drain their water deep down into the earth, so that you will get no benefit from it."

The very next day was struck by calamity. All the fruits were destroyed. The gardener wrung his hands with grief at all that he had spent on them, for the vines had tumbled down upon their trellises. On seeing this he realised his mistake and cried, "Would that I had served no other gods besides my Lord!"

This story is meant to teach believers never to speak proudly, but to say in all humility, "Whatever Allah has ordained must surely come to pass: there is no power save with Allah."

ﷺ *Alayhis Salum* 'May peace be upon him.'
The customary blessing on the prophets.